AF428104

How Do Animals Help the Forest Grow?

Animal Books for Kids 9-12 | Children's Animal Books

We know that animals live in the forest, little ones like chipmunks and big ones like bears. But did you know that animals help keep the forest healthy? Read on and find out how!

FORESTS AND ANIMALS NEED EACH OTHER

The plants and the animals of a forest are all part of the same ecosystem. They nourish each other and help each other in surprising ways. Animals use leaves and twigs from plants to build their nests. They dig under the bark of trees to eat insects that would otherwise hurt the tree.

Eagle in Nest

Black Mole

Burrowing animals and insects dig through the ground, loosening the soil. That makes it easier for plant roots to find their way to water. Trees convert carbon dioxide into oxygen, which animals need to breathe!

As much as animals need plants for food and shelter, plants need animals to disperse their seeds and cut down on damaging pests. It's a system that has grown up over hundreds of thousands of years.

Squirrel

Humans, however, have a different relationship with both forests and animals. We tend to see forests as a resource to cut down and turn into firewood, furniture, or houses; and we tend to see the animals of the forest as either dangerous monsters or potential food.

If we were not so good at what we do, the ecosystem could absorb us as it absorbs bears and ants and all sorts of other creatures. But we are very good at hunting the animals and harvesting the trees, and we are putting whole ecosystems at risk.

Koala

ANIMALS KEEP THE FOREST HEALTHY

In the natural world, there is a food chain. Bigger animals eat smaller animals, which themselves eat even smaller animals. The animals that are not meat eaters get their food from plants. When the animals die, their nutrients return to the soil or the water, nourishing the plants, and the cycle starts again.

In the middle of the food chain are creatures like birds, bats, and lizards that consume insects. These creatures eat enough insects to help keep the insect population from overrunning the plants. A healthy population of creatures in this range can keep what the insects do under control, and let the forest develop in a healthy way. If these creatures are not present—if, for instance, hunting and pesticides kill the birds—then you can have a storm of insects that attack the trees and that the trees cannot resist.

In tropical rainforests, the seeds of many trees need animals to eat their fruit and carry the seeds away from the tree. Fruit that falls directly under the tree and sprouts there is like a salad bar for insects and small rodents that are waiting for it. The seeds that travel with an animal away from the parent tree, and then sprout where the animal poops them out, have a much better chance of survival.

As wild animal populations reduce, the trees that rely on them to carry their seeds get fewer. The trees that spread their seed in the

wind or by water are more successful, and this changes the balance of the forest.

Deers

The key to a healthy forest is lots of interactions between animals and animals, animals and plants, and plants and plants. When you remove any participant, all the interactions suffer and the forest gets weaker.

WHERE FORESTS ARE SUFFERING

Here are some examples where removing animals from a forest has made a forest weaker. In a few cases, people have been able to return animals to the ecosystem and strengthen the forest again.

The Waterfalls of Chamarel

MAURITIUS

The island of Mauritius is off the east coast of Africa. Its forests depended on large, fruit-eating animals like tortoises, giant lizards, and also birds to eat their fruit and distribute their seeds.

Europeans first settled on Mauritius in the 1600s. They soon hunted the large animals to extinction. This weakened the forests of the whole island, reducing the ability of the fruiting trees to create new generations. The original Mauritian forest only exists now in a few protected areas, and the rest of the island has invasive species.

Mauritius

Tortoise

Conservationists have introduced large tortoises from other islands, and they have helped save an ebony tree that is native to Mauritius. Saplings of the tree do not survive if they sprout and try to grow too close to their parent. The tortoises eat the fruit of the tree and then poop the seeds out far away from the adult trees as they move around the landscape.

CENTRAL AFRICAN REPUBLIC

In the Ngotto Forest of the Central African Republic, extensive hunting had cut down the population of large animals. This means that the spread of trees that depend on the seeds passing through an animal has gotten much less, while the species of trees that have wind-borne seeds are increasing.

Star Fruit

This changes the whole nature of the forest. Large-seed trees like the cola nut and the African star apple are declining and may disappear altogether if there are no animals to eat their fruit, process their seeds, and distribute them.

HAWAII

Hawaii used to have large land animals, including the moa-nalo, a flightless duck with a bill like a tortoise. It became extinct after people from Polynesia settled in Hawaii over one thousand years ago. The moa-nalo seems to have behaved and eaten like a tortoise, performing for Hawaii what the tortoises on Mauritius do to process the seeds of large-seed fruiting trees. Scientists want to introduce giant tortoises to help create the conditions to protect and perhaps restore some of Hawaii's remaining original forest.

Hawaii

Agouti

COASTAL BRAZIL

The agouti is a large rodent that eats fruit and buries seeds in the rainforest of Brazil's Atlantic coast. As hunting reduces the population of agouti, the number of new seedlings of a local species of palm tree has reduced.

UGANDA

In Uganda, the krobodua tree has large fruit that the forest elephants eat. They distribute the seed of the krobodua so there are new seedlings. As hunting cuts down the population of forest elephants, the number of new krobodua trees is declining each year.

Tapir

CENTRAL BRAZIL

The tapir is a forest mammal that has flourished in the rainforests of Brazil. It contributes to the forest with its dung, out of which sprout palm tree seedlings from the palm fruit the tapir has eaten. People hunt tapirs for their meat, and are cutting down the rainforest for wood, which reduces their habitat. As the number of tapirs goes down, new palm tree seedlings also get fewer.

MEXICO

In Mexico, spider monkeys enjoy the fruit of the sapodilla tree, and spread its seeds through the Zona Maya. When logging cuts up the forest into isolated patches, destroying the habitat, the monkeys disappear and there are no new sapodilla trees.

Spider Monkey

Acacia Tree

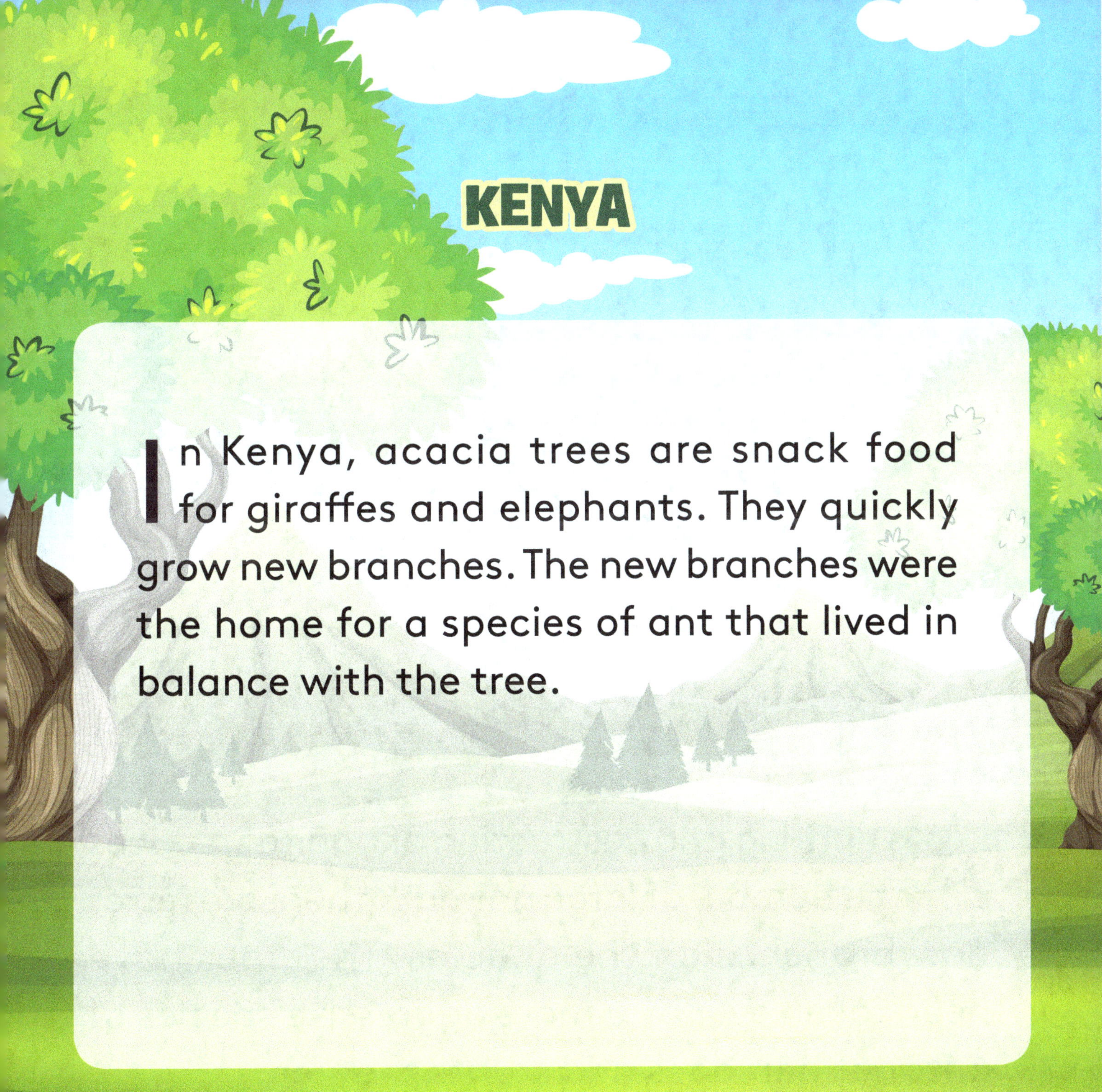

KENYA

In Kenya, acacia trees are snack food for giraffes and elephants. They quickly grow new branches. The new branches were the home for a species of ant that lived in balance with the tree.

As hunting and destruction of habitat reduces the number of large animals, there are fewer new branches on the acacias. The trees have been taken over by a more aggressive species of ant that damages and stunts the tree.

In the areas where there are no more large animals, the grass flourishes and grows tall. The grass provides a home for huge populations of African mice and other rodents.

Rodent

The small animals carry fleas that can transmit bubonic plague and other diseases to humans. For more about serious diseases and how they spread, read the Baby Professor book The Deadliest Diseases in History. So humans, and not just plants, can suffer when the large animals are removed from the forest.

In 1938 the United States created Olympic National Park to preserve an example of the original North American forest. However, eliminating wolves and other predators has let the population of deer and elk skyrocket.

Olympic National Park

The ruminants over-eat shoots and young trees, causing unexpected damage. For instance, if the deer over-graze along the banks of streams and rivers, the river banks can collapse and the streams can change their course. If there are no young trees to replace the mature ones, the forest will eventually die. The forest is very different now than it was 80 years ago.

Reintroducing wolves can help control the number of elk and deer, and protect the younger trees in the forest. With more young

trees growing along the edges of streams, the banks stabilize and the streams stay in the their courses.

TAKING CARE OF OUR WORLD

We can't just treat the world as if all the things in it will never run out. Lots of plants and animals have become extinct because of human activity, and lots of forests and animal species are under threat. Climate change and global warming add to the stresses on those who share this Earth with us.

Read Baby Professor books like Endangered Mammals from Around the World; Vulnerable, Endangered, and Critically Endangered Animals; and What Every Child Should Know about Climate Change to understand more about the pressures on our animals, our world, and ourselves.

Visit

BABY PROFESSOR
EDUCATION KIDS

www.BabyProfessorBooks.com
to download Free Baby Professor eBooks and view
our catalog of new and exciting Children's Books